CHOSEN

From Party Girl To Jesus Girl

Sue-Ann Montaque

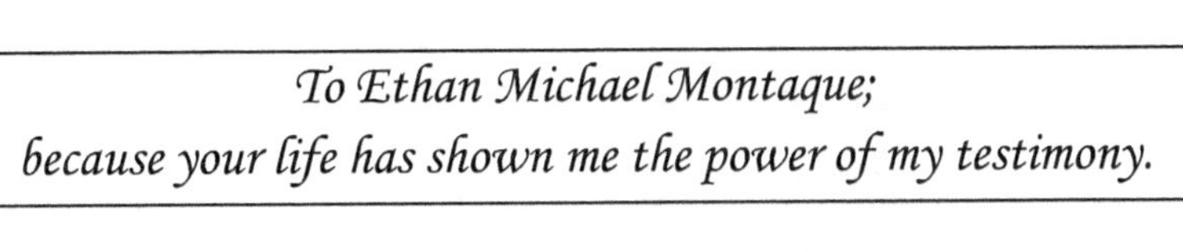
To Ethan Michael Montaque;
because your life has shown me the power of my testimony.

Acknowledgments

There are some amazing persons without whom this book would not be possible.

C. Orville McLeish and the HCP Book Publishing team: thank you for your amazing support and for making this book possible.

A Special Thank You:

To my Lord, Saviour, and King, Jesus Christ, for Your never-ending love, grace, and enabling power. Thank You for showing me who I am: a beloved daughter, a Jesus Girl.

To Tahnida Nunes, prayer warrior, prophet, and friend, thank you for always praying me through and believing in me. You were the first person to ever prophesy into my life. I love you.

To Bishop Christine Haber, you are love on two feet. Thank you for activating me and for loving me as Jesus loves me. You have been the conduit for so many significant milestones in my life. You are so special to me. I love you with all my heart.

To Pastor Fitzroy Kerr, thank you for being my spiritual father and believing in me when I did not believe in myself. You pushed me out of my comfort zone, and now I can fly. I love you so much.

To Pastor Gina York, beloved sister, friend, and mentor. God knew I needed you in my life for such a time as this. You are one of my biggest cheerleaders; I love you so BIG.

To my PDM family, a special thanks to my beloved Sis. Nov, Sis. Kadie, Rovy, Pastor Orrett, and so many others who continue to encourage and hold me up in prayer. I really could not have done this without you.

To my wonderful family, my precious Ethan, mom Arlene, dad Horace, Damian, Tricia, and my sweet Malachi and Dayna. You are the inspiration behind me sharing my story. I thank God that He has changed our family's story, and I pray that many families and other lives will be blessed by the miracle of Jesus Christ in their homes and lives.

Table of Contents

Preface

What is my purpose? Only four words, but this is the most powerful question you may ever ask yourself. As a young woman growing up and struggling with my identity, the answer to that question eluded me. There were so many times in my life when I felt like I was not enough and purposeless. I tried finding fulfillment in so many different places, and I would run to relationships to fill that void. I can definitely relate to many of the women in the Bible who encountered Jesus Christ in their brokenness. I feel such a burden on my heart; there are many women right now who are hurting and struggling with their self-worth, identity, and feeling that they are not enough.

The world tells us that to have worth, we must prove that we are good enough through the eyes of man by having things like a good hairstyle with a great wardrobe, jobs, a good body, and a whole host of other things. I continued to search for peace, wholeness, and a sense of stability, and I ended up searching in all the wrong places that did not give me the freedom or stability I was looking for.

Then, like the broken women I can relate to in the Bible, I met Jesus, and my life has never been the same. This book is a love story written by the Lover of my soul long before I was even formed in my mother's womb. Come with me on a journey as this book tells how a lost, broken woman was saved and set free by the power of love, by being *Chosen: From Party Girl To Jesus Girl.*

Key Text

1 Timothy 1:12-17 - NLT

I thank Christ Jesus our Lord, who has given me strength to do his work. He considered me trustworthy and appointed me to serve him, even though I used to blaspheme the name of Christ. In my insolence, I persecuted his people. But God had mercy on me because I did it in ignorance and unbelief. Oh, how generous and gracious our Lord was! He filled me with the faith and love that come from Christ Jesus. This is a trustworthy saying, and everyone should accept it: "Christ Jesus came into the world to save sinners"—and I am the worst of them all. But God had mercy on me so that Christ Jesus could use me as a prime example of his great patience with even the worst sinners. Then others will realize that they, too, can believe in him and receive eternal life. All honor and glory to God forever and ever! He is the eternal King, the unseen one who never dies; he alone is God. Amen.

The Letter

I jumped out of my sleep, gasping for breath. I looked around, feeling a sense of disorientation, expecting to see the scene I just came out of. Then I remembered feeling such a sense of relief; it was just a dream. I dreamt that my mother had stabbed my father to death. In the dream, she had given him three stab wounds; I remember crying out to her asking her why she did it. There was something very different about this dream; it was so vivid, and as my day went on, I could not shake it. I went to work that day, and the dream still did not leave. I was led to share it with a friend who was a devout woman of God and she shared her testimony of how the Lord spoke to her about forgiving her father through a dream. While she was speaking, the Lord ministered to me, and I realized this was something I had to pray through.

I began to talk to the Lord about the dream and decided that I would seek the Lord's face in prayer about it when I got home. While in prayer, the Lord gave me instructions to write an open and honest letter to my father, basically baring my heart to him about how I felt about everything that happened in our family over the years, but, most importantly, I was to forgive him. I remember telling the

Holy Spirit that He would have to write this letter because this was bigger than me.

I grew up in a very emotionally abusive home. I did not see love between my mother and father, so I did not know what a loving marriage looked like. My father always provided for us financially and, in my earlier years, I do remember having a closer relationship with my dad. We would always have birthday parties to celebrate my brother's birthday as well as mine. We would go out for family dinners on a Friday, and I would always go and kiss my daddy on his cheek every night before I went to bed. I loved my father, but as we got older, things began to change. I became more aware of the tension between my mom and dad, and that began to spill over into the relationship with us as the children. Things continued to worsen, and I remember the night I decided I would not kiss my dad on his cheek before going to bed anymore. Our family continued to grow even more distant, and my dad was not there for us emotionally. I remember feeling like in order to receive his love, I had to perform, so I started to believe that receiving love was performance-based. I learned emotional suppression very early on, and that ended my dreams of ever growing up knowing what it was like to be a daddy's girl, or so I thought.

As I began to write the letter, the Holy Spirit began to download what the dream meant, and He began to give me the words to write. He wrote about things I did not realize I still had in my memory bank, like old pieces of furniture covered with fabric and dust that was now being uncovered, being dusted off and brought out into the light. As I wrote, the Lord showed me a vision of a very bad wound. He explained that when we go to the doctor with a wound, the first thing the doctor does is clean the wound to remove the surface dirt, then he uses an antiseptic, and, oh how painful the application of the antiseptic is: it burns. The application of the antiseptic removes all the germs that could make the wound infected in the future. Then he dresses the wound and will prescribe any medications and follow up treatments as needed for the wound to heal properly. If treated correctly, the wound will heal properly, leaving only a scar as a reminder of what happened, but it will not cause any additional pain. The Lord said to me in that moment, "This is what I have come to do in your life, daughter. I have come to heal and restore all that was lost to you. If you obey Me, I will give you all, not just for you but for your family's sake and generations to come."

"I will repay you for the years the locusts have eaten, the great locust and the young locust, the other locusts and the locust swarm, my great army that I sent among you." (Joel 2:25 – NIV).

It took a few days for the letter to be completed, but when it was finished, I felt like ten tons had been lifted off me.

I felt free! As I went to print the letter, the Lord instructed me to make one copy for my father and make a copy for my mother. I followed His instruction and made two copies. I left a copy of my letter on my mother's bed (she was away at the time and would find it waiting for her on her return), and I called my dad and asked him to stop by for something.

A few days later, I received a text message from my dad thanking me and admitting that only the leading of the Lord could have made me write such a letter to him. He received my words and told me he would reflect deeply on what I had said and try to make amends. I was blown away! I would never have thought at the age of thirty-nine years old that any kind of change could come to my family, that it could be restored, and yet here was God breathing new life into my family. Unknown to me, this was only the beginning of God's rescue and restoration mission for me.

Chapter 1

The Beginning

I did not feel chosen for most of my life. I did not feel like much of anything, to be honest. Self-worth was an unknown paradigm to me, and so very often, I would find myself asking these questions: "Who am I? What is my purpose? Why am I here?" I would find myself facing these questions quite often in my childhood and growing up into my teenage and adult years.

I grew up in a small, very sheltered family with my mom, father, and older brother, and, as a little girl, I could not quite figure out just where I fit in. I do remember being a very loving and sensitive child and I always felt happiest surrounded by the people I loved. What I did not know then was that stability would be a constantly moving bullseye whose target I would continue to miss well into my late thirties. While other little girls were busy dreaming about being powerful career women, I dreamed about marrying my dream husband and becoming a housewife who would take care of our home and children. Family, love, and security were the things I dreamed about, and I believed they would have brought me peace and joy.

At two years old, I was diagnosed as a chronic asthmatic, and throughout my life, I was constantly in and out of hospital. It is amazing to know that even then, the Lord had His hand on my life, and He knew His plan for me was to live and not die and to declare what He has done. He gave His angels charge over me, and one such angel was my mother. She was always taking care of me; always so diligent in her care for me. She knew my illness inside out, and she never left my side. There was one particular time when I was not feeling well, and Mommy knew that something was not right. She told my dad that she felt that something was wrong, so they both rushed me to the hospital's emergency room, and I overheard the doctors telling my mother that my lungs had collapsed and if she had waited one moment longer, I would have died. I had so many close encounters with death throughout my life.

I did not realize then that the enemy was using this illness as one of the many ways to plant seeds of fear in my life from an early age. I started to question, "Why wasn't I born normal?" In Jamaican language, "How come my lungs neva mek good?" Something as basic as breathing, I could not even do that properly, and it always left me wondering if today would be the "day" when I would not make it. My self-esteem took a huge beating. The diagnosis of asthma also introduced steroids as a part of my treatment, which caused massive weight gain. The nick-name "fatty boom boom," among other things, only opened the door for an unhealthy relationship with food and an overall destructive view of my body, my image, and a further hit to my self-esteem. I took on the spirit of shyness, and I only felt comfortable remaining close to my trusted tribe of two friends or my mother. Being around people became unbearable, and this spirit of shyness would later lead to me developing a crippling fear of public speaking or doing anything that made me the center of attention. I did not believe that anyone would want to speak to me or hear what I had to say. I did not know that these were lies; seeds being planted by the enemy to destroy my purpose. I continued to grow up believing the lie that my worth was directly related to how I looked or what I could do. What a lie!

As I got older and entered into my early teen years, my mother and father's relationship continued to deteriorate with their marital disagreements, and my home life took a turn for the worse. The spirit of rejection continued to reign over me, along with shyness and fear. I stopped caring about everything in life. I hated my family, and I hated my life. I soon realized that another spirit had come along to join the party: the spirit of people-bondage. People's acceptance became so important to me and was now added as one of life's mission for me. I did not care where it came from; I just knew I had to find acceptance hoping it would fill the gaping hole that was in my heart.

As I entered my third year of high school, I found acceptance in friendships at school, and I stopped focusing totally on school. I began skipping classes and found myself in places I was not supposed to be. Then I got the news that I had to repeat my third year at the end of the school year. What a smack in the face! Again, the hand of the Lord showed up, and something inside me knew that no matter what was happening around me or what I was going through, if I became a failure, it would all be on me. Then came the spirit of control. I decided I would now control my life, and I would take whatever I wanted in life, including excelling in anything I put my mind to. Suddenly I found a new wind and went on to excel in high school. I was bestowed the honor of becoming a prefect and a top performer in my exams. I did so well in my CXC exams and got a perfect 100% pass in Math that the CXC council thought I had cheated and decided to hold on to my grades.

Again, the Lord gave me yet another glimpse that His hand was on my life and as my mother joined her faith with His, they fought for me. My principal took me into 6th form on faith with no CXC results, so I moved on to study the sciences in the sixth form. Later in the school year, my CXC passes were eventually released to me. As I look back on that experience, I realize the Lord used it to bring me closer to my mother, and it would be yet another test that would become a testimony.

While I continued to excel academically, I began to explore the party scene when I turned sixteen, and I loved it. My mother was a woman of God, and although she made sure we went to church every Sabbath, I still did not have my own personal relationship with God. I grew up fearing Him, but I decided to seek the world instead at this pivotal age of sixteen. I started hanging out with friends and going to all the clubs and sessions; I was hooked. I found my new love, and partying became my greatest joy. Each party felt like the next high, and I found that there was a temporary enjoyment and release from my brokenness. So, as we say in Jamaica, every drum that beat, I was there. I loved the music, and I loved to dance. I felt free when I was partying. I have always loved music and dancing; my father was a member of a sound system when he was younger, and we had a massive sound system at home. He had tons of records, and I would look forward to Sunday evenings when he tuned up the sound system and played his old records. He taught me how to use the turntable, and I even got my own portable turntable that allowed me to play his records on my own time. I had no idea that I was really a worshipper, and my love for music was a gift that God would use to connect me to Him.

I would love to say that the music and dancing were the only things I loved about the party scene, but it was not. I also began to really enjoy the attention from the boys that I was getting. I grew up in a very sheltered home, so this was new to me, especially since I grew up feeling rejected and had low self-esteem.

By now, I was no longer on steroids, and I had developed an eating disorder where I was starving myself, so I had grown into a very tall, lean, and attractive young woman. I had really long, lean legs, and the shorter and more revealing the clothes, the better it was for me. This newfound attention felt good; I wanted to attract attention to my body because it validated me. It was one of the only times I felt I had self-worth outside of my academic accomplishments. It also gave me a sense of control as well. I did not know anything at that time about the scriptures or the Word of God. For example, it says in Jeremiah 1:5:

"Before I formed you in the womb I knew you, before you were born I set you apart." (NIV).

The brokenness I felt from my family and home persuaded me to try and find my value and worth in other things: men, alcohol, cigarettes, and partying. That became my life. I thank God that even though I was broken and pursuing the world, He still pursued me. He is a God who will leave the ninety-nine for the one every time. I praise Him that He is a God who restores. I went on to college and graduated with honours at the top of my class, which landed me a job on the opening team of a brand-new luxury hotel. Was my life finally taking the turn I had been dreaming of?

Chapter 2
A New Life

I went on to do extremely well in my studies, but it was a completely different story at home. I could not control things there, and it continued to be excruciating living in my parents' home. I was partying really hard: drinking, smoking, and clubbing every chance I got. I would go to school, and on weekends and holidays, I would get dressed, go partying, come back the next morning, sleep all day, and the cycle would continue.

After graduating from university, I got the news that I had struck gold. One of the world's premiere, luxury hotels was breaking ground in Jamaica. It was the first of its kind on our island but, the best part was, it would be opening in Montego Bay. My home life felt like a prison. Here was my chance at freedom, my chance to find happiness, to finally be able to BREATHE! I felt like God had given me a ticket to get away, and I was not going to pass up the opportunity. I put in my application, passed their rigorous selection process and, in a few months, I was making plans to move to Montego Bay with my college mates. I will never forget the letter my mother wrote to me on the day I was leaving home; it still brings tears to my eyes. I know something died in her that day; she was being left alone to bear the sadness that resided in our home, like an all too familiar friend. Even with that knowledge, it could not make me stay. I had to escape.

We packed my belongings into a truck and made our way to Montego Bay to begin my new life, or so I thought. I remember walking into the house I would be sharing with my roommates, and I could not contain my excitement. It was really happening; I was finally free. My new life had begun, and I felt renewed hope rising on my inside, like inflating a bubble that was about to burst. I remember we celebrated our first night of being on our own at one of the hotel's welcome parties. By then, I was a seasoned party girl, and I had a ball partying, getting to know my new found friends, and enjoying my new found life. I quickly found favor in the eyes of my superiors and began to climb the culinary ranks very rapidly. I did not know then but would find out later that there was a Joseph anointing on my life.

"The Lord was with Joseph so that he prospered, and he lived in the house of his Egyptian master." (Genesis 39:2 – NIV).

I continued to excel in my career, taking the culinary industry by storm. I was also entering competitions on behalf of my hotel in Jamaica. I began to travel and represent my hotel, not only in Jamaica, but I would go on to represent the Caribbean and the Atlantic region in a number of international competitions. It felt like I was living somebody else's life. Traveling, being chauffeured around in limousines, eating eight-course 5-star meals with some of the biggest names in the food industry, and cooking for them all seemed so surreal. I still saw myself as that shy, insecure, rejected, and broken little girl, and, yet, here I was, becoming the very thing I had never dreamed of becoming: a powerful career woman.

Although my career was going full steam ahead, my personal life was the complete opposite. I was still a train wreck emotionally, and even though I had dated a number of men, I found no peace. The gaping hole in my heart continued to get bigger and wider as I moved from one failed relationship to the next. I continued wearing the mask of my achievements as a pretense that I was in control and had it all together. It felt like it was working for a while. No one knew the battle that was raging beneath my broad smile and positive, outgoing demeanor. I continued to make one mistake after another in my personal life; I continued the partying, drinking, smoking, and the boyfriends, but still no peace and no signs of stability on the horizon in my personal life.

As if the dysfunction in my personal life was not enough, lurking in the background, I continued to starve myself, having developed an eating disorder from my childhood weight gain. I did not care about the damage I was doing to my body; all I cared about was ensuring I kept myself looking the way I wanted.

I remember having a fainting spell one day right before dinner service started. One minute I was picking spices off the service rack, and the next minute I went crashing into the rack. It would actually be hilarious had it not been for the fact that I could have fainted on the hot range and gotten seriously injured, but that did not stop me from starving myself. The hole in my heart continued to grow deeper. I continued to go about my routine until one day something happened or, should I say, someone caught my attention. What do you know; there was a new kid on the block.

Chapter 3

A Dream Come True: Saying Yes To The Dress

The new kid on the block turned out to be an amazing young man, and we were paired to work together. We grew close over time, and we confided in each other about our other half as we were both in relationships. There just seemed to be something about this new kid on the block that intrigued me. As time went on, I thought: "Yes, he gets me. He's the one." We both decided to end our current relationships to be together. We decided to get married, and then I found out I was pregnant with our son, Ethan. We continued with our plans and, surrounded by family and friends, we got married and started a new life together. We welcomed our precious son, Ethan, into the world seven months later, and I felt like my life had finally come together. I felt happy, and I felt like I had finally found the elusive peace I searched for my whole life.

Unfortunately, that peace did not last very long. An overseas job opportunity came up, and my husband went away for a while. The separation was unbearable, and I felt rejected all over again, but this time with a young baby. I knew my husband loved us, but we could not see eye to eye on the matter, and our marriage went downhill from there. It was not long before my old patterns emerged, and I began seeing someone else. I did not know that rejection is a spirit, so I searched for comfort in someone else. When my husband came back and tried to make amends, my heart was already hardened; it was stone cold towards him, and I had no interest in making things right with him. We officially separated and went our separate ways.

After my marriage failed, I became a broken, single mother to a broken young son. I remember praying to God and asking Him for yet another husband, asking Him for a father for my son, asking for the right relationship, the right job, the right anything. I thought if I could just get the right thing from God, everything would be better, and this ever-deepening emptiness I felt in my heart would surely go away. I continued to pray these prayers for years.

After spending six years in Montego Bay, I decided to move back home to Kingston to be close to my family to make it easier to raise my son. The new man I was seeing also lived in Kingston, so this made it easier for us to date. Unfortunately, this relationship did not last either. Being truly honest with myself, I had no business being in a relationship with someone when I had not even taken the time to heal from my failed marriage. There were other failed relationships along the way as I struggled to find peace, including a failed reconciliation attempt with my ex-husband, which brought my son and I even more heartache. My son and I would spend years trying to build a stable and happy life, and there were times when we almost did not make it, but then a miracle happened.

One Friday evening, I had an encounter with another man that rocked me to my very core and would shift how I saw myself, how I saw relationships, and how I saw my life. Could it be that this time around, I had finally found the one?

Chapter 4
The Encounter: The One

It was a Friday evening, and I was at the end of my rope. I could not keep living like this: I felt empty, beaten down, and depressed; I did not want to live anymore. I just could not deal with all the dysfunction, not just in my own life, but in my family's life as well. I found myself pacing my bedroom floor, "God, where are You? Why is my brother sick? How much longer will we have to go through this? Why is my life such a mess? When will I ever be happy? Are You hearing me?" Then I uttered words I will never forget: "I don't want to live anymore, but if You're real, reveal Yourself to me, and I will surrender my life to You forever." I do not know what happened next, but I knew that a presence filled my bedroom, and I was on my knees, flat on the floor. I became enveloped in a warmth I had never felt before, and a wave of peace flooded my soul. It was greater than any alcoholic buzz I had ever had in my life. I knew I was having an encounter with God, and, for the first time, I fell in love. For the first time, I felt love: true, pure love. My heart was wrecked, and I began to weep in a way I had never wept before. I immediately knew that something supernatural had taken place in my room on this ordinary but not so ordinary Friday evening, and I had been changed.

That Sunday, I went to the church I had been visiting at the time and told them I needed to be baptized right away. They were well ahead into their baptism class, but I told them I could not wait for the next round and needed to be added right away. They recognized that I would not take no for an answer, so I was given a crash course in what this new commitment would mean in my life. Baptism was on for the upcoming Sunday and an elder agreed to do a quick review with me on one of the evenings during the week leading up to the baptism. My transformation felt a lot like Saul's when he met Jesus on the Damascus road and became Paul. I also realized that even though I had made a decision to turn to the world at age sixteen, seeds had already been sown in my heart; all those times my mother ensured that we went to church to hear the Word of God, now God was bringing the increase.

On Sunday, July 10, 2011, my family and friends came to witness my commitment to the Lord in water baptism. Had I finally become someone's girl? A Jesus girl?

Chapter 5

Jesus Girl: Not Quite

After making the confession of Jesus Christ and getting baptized, I ended things with my boyfriend because I did not want to continue having sex outside of marriage. I started serving in my church and got involved in the hospitality ministry, home care groups, and the young women's mentorship ministry. Although I was growing in my faith, there continued to be a struggle with my sexuality. It was still an area of my life that I had not yet fully surrendered to the Lord. I still struggled with men. I knew I was growing in the things of God, but I still had a desire for earthly companionship. I did not realize that I made the dream I had as a little girl become an idol in my life. I had continued with the mindset that until I had the husband and the family that I dreamed of, my life would not be whole or complete, even as a Christian. I knew I loved Jesus, but I still wanted my man and a family. Can I get an AMEN somebody!

Seriously though, the enemy still had access to my life through my heart and mind. If I am completely honest, I did not trust God in this area of my life, and I did not trust Him with my relationships. I watched all my friends around me get married, and I was still unmarried and waiting. My mind was not renewed in this area, so I was still the little girl who was rejected by her father or the young party girl who was still trying to fix a wounded heart with the attention I gained from guys. The Lord showed me later on that this was an open door for the enemy to attack my identity, just as he did when I was a little girl, because I thought my value was found in a man when really, I did not know who I was. My heart needed to be completely healed, and I needed deliverance in this area of my life.

I continued to serve the Lord, yet got involved in ungodly relationships. It was very easy for the enemy to come back in and crush me again in this area of my life. Not only was I hurt all over again dating these men, but it also put me in a deep, backslidden condition. Although I was in a fallen state, I found myself being amazed once again. What amazed me was not the fact that I found myself in this position again, but I was amazed at God's grace and mercy. Do you know what Jesus did? Jesus came riding in, again, showing me that His hand was upon my life. How did Jesus do that? Well, it seems as though my beloved Saviour likes to change the course of my life on Friday evenings.

I was involved in another ungodly relationship, and on another Friday evening, I heard the Lord speak to me clearly. He said, "End this relationship NOW!" I remember that moment like it was yesterday. What was so amazing about it was even though I wrote the "now" in caps, God did not shout the word at me; He spoke to me with such a gentle and quiet authority, but I heard the power in His voice. I agreed immediately; I did not fight it; I did not argue. I made arrangements to speak to the guy I was dating, and I broke it off and did not look back.

After breaking up with him, things got tough. I remember coming home one evening, just two weeks into our separation. I went down on my knees in prayer, and I began to weep. I wept bitterly; my heart was so broken, again. I was in such a backslidden state; I remember just being angry at God and asking Him why? Why was it so wrong for me to want to be in a relationship? Why was it so wrong for me wanting to have someone to love me? I remember His presence filling my room, and with such tenderness, the Lord asked me a question: "Am I not enough? Why is a relationship with a man such an idol in your heart? Have I not done enough for you? Have I not done all for you?" Those words stopped me in my tracks. I had been so consumed with what I wanted all these years that even being a Christian, I had never asked God what He wanted. For the first time, I decided to ask Him the question, "What do You want, Lord?" His response was simple, "Your heart." The Lord began to show me that I had never asked Him about who to date. I never brought this part of my life or this part of my heart to Him. I never shared the desire in my heart to be connected to another human being in a marriage with the Lord. I prayed to Him about it and asked Him to give me a husband, to give me a family, and the reasons why I wanted those things, but I never surrendered that desire in my heart to the Lord.

The Lord showed me that He was the one who placed that desire there in the first place, but He did not want me to desire the desire more than desiring Him. That is what I had been doing all along. The Lord showed me that it was coming from a deeply rooted place. I really just wanted to be loved for who I was. As He continued to minister to my heart, I heard Him say, "You know My love, but now I want you to accept My love because you are made complete in Me. I made you; you are perfect, and I love you just the way you are." And no, I am not talking about the Billy Joel song.

I wept like a baby at the revelation the Lord was taking me into and, in that moment, I felt something shift in my heart. Something changed that night, and I repented before the Lord; my heart turned towards God for the first time in this area of my life. I gave the Lord my idol of marriage and my sexuality right then. I gave Him my whole heart. I allowed Him to touch that place in my heart that needed healing. In my first encounter, He showered me with His love. In this encounter, I allowed Him full access to my heart, and as my whole heart turned towards Him, I began my journey of recommitment to Jesus, and my journey to becoming a Jesus Girl began.

"I am my beloved's and His desire is toward me." (Song of Solomon 7:10 - KJV).

Chapter 6

Recommitment: New Beginnings

So now I am a Jesus girl. "Now what, Lord?" I would ask. If I said the next couple of weeks, even the next couple of months, were easy, I would be lying. The first couple of weeks were so rough. Instead of trying to drown my heartache in finding another earthly man, I ran to the feet of Jesus. I began journaling again, and I would pour my heart out to Jesus.

There was a point when I got angry at God, and I asked Him why it hurt so bad; why had He allowed me to get involved in these ungodly relationships, and now I was dealing with the aftermath of heartbreak and loneliness. The Lord quietly ministered to my heart in those moments, and, after drying my tears, I heard Him gently reminding me, "Daughter, I never told you to get involved in those relationships. I have better for you, but first you need to know that I am enough for you. I will heal your heart, and I will fill you with My Spirit." I could sense that the Lord had taken me to a new place. I could sense that I was getting closer to Him, and things were different this time. I could hear His voice much clearer now that I had given my whole heart to Him and, even though I was hurting, I felt His loving arms; I felt comforted. Even though I was in pain, somehow, I knew I would be okay.

Things started to get better in my relationship with Jesus, and as I continued growing in my relationship with Him, I was also growing in my career. I was now working at a new company and received a promotion earlier on in my tenure there. I was then offered another promotion that would relocate me to the 7th floor. I did not realize what God was doing at the time. As a little girl growing up, the number seven had always been my number. Growing up ignorant in the things of the Spirit, I was unaware that the number seven is God's holy number and represents God's divine completion. Again, God's mighty hand was at work in my life, and not even my ignorance could sway His plans for me.

I moved to the 7th floor and continued working in my new position, and God helped me overcome many hurdles. I continued to see God's favor on my life and in my career, and I once again found myself being offered yet another promotion, this time in a regional capacity. This would mean much more responsibility, and it should have also included a salary increase. Due to the increased responsibilities, I moved over to sit with the team that managed the regional operation.

As the days went by, things began to unravel, and it became clearer to me that things were just not what they seemed. Work progressed, and I then received the news that instead of giving me a salary increase, the company had decided to pay me a stipend instead. Things just did not seem right, and I found myself asking God what was happening. After being told that I would only be paid a stipend, I went home that evening, and I heard the Lord speak to me. He said, "Move your seat and go and sit with your people." I thought God's instruction meant I should go and sit with my Jamaica team at work. I later learnt this was all a divine set up orchestrated by God.

The moving of my seat was also tied intricately to Him moving me to the seventh floor. In moving my seat, I ended up sitting in front of and reconnecting with Tahnida, an old college friend who was now a Christian and an Evangelist. Little did I know how instrumental she would be in me recommitting my life to the Lord and stepping into my calling. She was the dear friend who shared her testimony with me when I told her about my dream that kick-started this restoration process. That night, I shared with my mom what the Lord had spoken to me about me moving my seat, and she asked me if I was sure this is what I wanted to do. I told her I believed the Lord had spoken, and I was going to obey. I had no idea that the Lord had put me on a journey to teach me the power of obeying one instruction that would open a door and change my life forever.

I woke up early the next morning, and I moved my seat and all my belongings and went to sit with the Jamaican team, and I ended up sitting in front of Tahnida. Things continued to go awry and got really intense at work. I found myself being sabotaged by people I trusted, and there was a definite war taking place spiritually. I remember one morning just going into work and feeling an intense need for prayer. The Holy Spirit knew I needed agreement, and He said, "Go to the woman of God." I remember that morning as if it were yesterday. I went to Tahnida and asked her to pray with me. She did not hesitate. We went into a meeting room, which incidentally was called Highgate, and closed the door. I told her what was happening, and as she began to pray for me, I felt something shift in my spirit. She began to prophesy over my life, telling me that I was a minister of the gospel, that I would have a global ministry, that God would use me mightily and that many souls would be won for the kingdom of God and that before I left this company, people would know that I was a woman of God. She also said that my son was a mighty man of God, and I should not forget or neglect him because he was great. I remember thinking to myself, "What is she talking about?" I still did not see that the Lord had a calling on my life. This was the first time I had anyone prophesy into my life. Nevertheless, from that day on, every time I wrote something, I would put it in a folder labeled "Minister Sue."

I continued to lean on the Lord, and I also had the support of Tahnida praying with and for me. The Lord brought me through the trials of work, and we gained the victory. He allowed me to build the support team for the region, and I was able to impact their lives for Jesus. I began to see the words Tahnida prayed over my life bear fruit as God continued to show up and show off in my life.

A month later, Tahnida invited me to a mentorship program being held by her Bishop, Bishop Christine Haber. She told me she had already written my name down in faith. I jumped on the opportunity immediately. Little did Tahnida know that I had been praying for a female mentor, a woman of God who could take me higher in the things of God. I began the mentorship program, and it was such an unbelievable blessing.

Two months into the program, I found myself praying one Saturday night, just thanking the Lord for His goodness. I remember saying to Him, "The only thing I would like to do now is recommit with water baptism." The next morning, I woke up to a message from Tahnida that she had a dream about me. I responded to her message, and she ended up telling me that Bishop was getting ready to baptize someone that day. She told me that Bishop had said the Lord told her she would be baptizing three persons, but, at the time, Bishop only knew who one of the persons would be. I knew immediately that I was one of the three based on my prayer the night before. Again it was only later that the Lord revealed to me that the number three represents resurrection. How could it be that I told the Lord I wanted to recommit my life in water baptism, and He opened the door for baptism the next day? Immediately, the Lord answered my prayer. What an amazing God! I wept.

I told Tahnida about my prayer the night before and asked her if I could come and be baptized. She said, "Of course." I jumped out of bed, got dressed, and made my way to Portmore.

On July 29, 2018, seven years after being baptized for the first time on July 10, 2011, I made a public declaration of my recommitment to Jesus, and my Bishop baptized me. True to His word, Bishop did indeed baptize three women that day; I was one of them. The Lord continued to work signs, wonders, and miracles in my life, and in August 2018, the Lord miraculously healed me from asthma. In one of Bishop's mentorship sessions, she requested anyone who wanted healing to step forward. We were instructed to lay our hands on the part of our bodies where we needed healing. I stepped forward and laid my hands on my chest. When Bishop laid her hands on my chest, anointing my chest with oil, she said, "The Lord said your faith has made you whole." I have not been afflicted with asthma again from that day onwards. It has been exactly two years and two months since I have been asthma free.

Chapter 7

Israel

I continued building my relationship with Jesus, and as I approached my fortieth birthday, I thought, "What better way to celebrate this milestone than to go to Italy." It was always my dream to travel to Italy. I always envisioned going there with my husband and eating our way through the different regions.

Forty was fast approaching and still no husband, so I called one of my close girlfriends, and we started making plans to go to Italy. The old Sue-Ann would have been sad that I had no husband to celebrate and accompany me to Italy for my birthday, but the love of Jesus had healed my heart, and I was just happy being able to live for Jesus. My girlfriend and I looked at the different tours, airfare, hotels, and I had just enough money saved up for our trip. I was so excited.

In May 2018, the Lord spoke to me saying, "You will not be going to Italy. I am sending you to Israel."

"Israel? Me, Lord? Really?" To say I was shocked would be an understatement because Israel was never on my radar. However, I said, "Okay, Lord, if You are sending me to Israel, then I will see the evidence." I did not give it another thought.

A month later, in June 2018, Tahnida told me she had already written my name down in faith to go with her ministry, CHMI, to Israel, so she was just officially extending the invitation to me, believing I would say yes. Just like that, a month later, after telling me He was sending me to Israel, the Lord opened the door for me to go.

As I continued walking with Him and preparing myself for the upcoming trip to Israel, I knew I needed a church home. I was still a member of the church that I had been baptized in 2011, but I had not been to church in over a year. I knew God was shifting me, so I continued to pray that God would lead me to the church home that He desired me to be in and to my shepherd.

One evening, my sister-in-law invited my mother and me to a meeting with her pastor at her church. Her pastor turned out to be a good family friend, Pastor Fitzroy Kerr. I first met Pastor Kerr seven years earlier at my current church. He came to speak at our New Year's Eve service. I remember hearing him speak and something shifted in my spirit. My mom happened to be with me at that New Year's Eve service, and, being a family friend, I begged her to introduce me to Pastor Kerr. I remember telling her I had to meet him, and I raced to meet him after service was over, pulling my poor mother along with me. Again, I did not know that this was yet another divinely orchestrated appointment that God had set up. God had just introduced me to my spiritual father and shepherd, and I did not even know it. Now, seven years later, I was at his church waiting to have a meeting with him, and, instead, I ended up staying throughout the entire service. During the service, I got the confirmation. I knew the Lord had led me to my home church. That night, they were also hosting a guest speaker, Pastor Gina York. I was introduced to her, and she was asked to pray for me. I chuckle now when I think about it. God truly is a great chess Master. Oh, how He moves the pieces of our lives and puts them together. I did not know that Pastor Gina would end up becoming a very dear friend, sister in Christ, and ministry partner. What a God of destiny.

I visited this church again on Sunday, and I never stopped going ever since. Two months later, Praise Deliverance Ministry became my new church home, and I was received into membership. I found my shepherd and my church family. I immediately began serving in the church and, one month later, just as Jesus promised, He filled me with His Spirit; I received the baptism of the Holy Spirit. Israel was fast approaching and, before I knew it, February 9, 2019 was here, and we were off to Israel, all twelve of us like the twelve apostles, called by Jesus to return to the holy land. It was such a surreal moment when my feet touched the soil of the holy land; to say that trip was life-changing would be an understatement. While in Israel, I learned how to read and speak Hebrew, and I also gained a new family. I have over two-thousand pictures of this amazing pilgrimage, and I will share more of this amazing experience when I write my book dedicated specifically to Israel.

Among the most precious memories for me in Israel was visiting the pool of Bethesda seven days into our stay, where the man was healed of his infirmity after thirty-eight years, just as I had been healed of my asthma after suffering with that disease for thirty-eight years. There was the life-altering moment of being baptized in the Jordan river again by Bishop Haber, having been baptized by her seven months earlier. Jesus told me while there that I was His chosen for such a time as this.

Another special moment was visiting the city of Magdala where Mary Magdalene was delivered from her demons, just as Jesus had delivered me from my demons and seeing Jesus look me in the eyes in that very city saying, "I know your name." We took communion in the garden tomb; we sailed on the Sea of Galilee; I climbed the mountain of En Gedi "David's Waterfall." David is such a beloved person in the Bible for me, and I could not believe that God allowed me to go and see with my own two eyes where David had been. Then, we walked the Via Dolorosa; the very route believed to have been taken by Christ through the Old City of Jerusalem to Calvary before His crucifixion.

As I walked in the steps of my Master, the revelation and gravity of His sacrifice was evident, and the beauty of His heart was revealed: He LOVES us, He LOVES people, He LOVES ME! The revelation of His love hit me like a ton of bricks; to think that He would send me to Israel to get a deeper revelation of who He is, not only for myself but also for those who, through my story, would have a deeper understanding of His love themselves. I realized it was never just about me. It has always been about Him and Him choosing to use my life for others to be impacted for His glory, according to His desire.

I was confronted by His love. I found in Jesus Christ the very thing I had been searching for all my life. It is amazing how the lens that we look through defines how we see love, but it does not reveal the truth of love. I did not know my identity, so my definition of love was directly linked to my identity; a broken identity and believing the lies of the enemy and what he said about who I was, equalling a counterfeit. That led me down a road to seek validation from the world, and that always left me even more wounded and broken than before.

Learning my identity in Christ now equaled me knowing true love. I can safely and truthfully say that it was the love of Christ that healed me, and it is the love of Christ that heals people.

"When Jesus heard it, He saith unto them, 'They that are whole have no need of the physician, but they that are sick: I came not to call the righteous but sinners to repentance.'" (Mark 2:17 – KJV).

There were so many dead things in my life, so many dreams, hopes, and desires that I thought would never come alive again, yet God rescued me from the clutches of death, from the hand of the enemy, and gave me new beginnings, not one, but many. He continues to restore and redeem me, and He will do the same for you. Jesus gave His life for us, and He will do a deep work in us. He has the power to get to the deep, hidden things because He comes to bring about complete healing. He desires for us to live the abundant life now, not for you to wait until you get to heaven. The abundant life is found in Him, and there is always more for you in Christ Jesus once you are still breathing.

Have you given up hope on your family, job, or life? What have you given up on? I pray that my story will encourage you to come to Jesus so He can give you a new life.

My testimony is a testimony of redemption. It is a testimony that through acceptance of God's grace and mercy, through Jesus Christ His Son, my life was transformed and changed. I received His free gift, the gift of His Son, the very treasure of heaven, and my life has never been the same. The feelings of being rejected, unwanted, unloved throughout my childhood have now been replaced with the everlasting love and hope I have found in Jesus. It was so important for the Lord to show me my identity in Christ and not the false one that the enemy had given me. That was a lie I had believed for far too long.

God chose to use everything in my life to accomplish His purpose and to turn my mess into a message, to use my test as testimonies of His grace and goodness. It is the love of God that has allowed me to have a story to tell. The Lord restored and redeemed me, and He also healed my relationship with my father and the relationships within my family. We are not perfect, but we have come a very far way, and God's grace has been so evident in our lives.

When you truly begin to see God and understand who He is, then you will begin to see yourself for who you really are. It has been almost four years since I have been celibate, and the Lord has kept me. I know now that my value is found in Him and who He has called me to be. I know now what it is to have the unconditional love of a father.

"Though my mother and my father forsake me, the Lord will receive me." (Psalm 27:10 – NIV).

I am Chosen; I am a Jesus Girl. What an amazing, life-changing revelation.

Afterword

God loves you, but you have a part to play.

In my quest to make sense of my life, God rescued me from the darkness, and I am so grateful for His love, mercy, and grace.

As I reflect on the many times that Jesus pulled me back from my destructive patterns, I can see that I also had a part to play. I had to respond to God's love for me and the invitation that He extended to me. The surrendering of my life and will was the display of my love for Jesus. Obedience is the display of our love for Jesus.

God always had a plan for my life. When I chose to participate in God's plan for my life, everything changed. The first step was surrendering to Jesus, admitting that I was a sinner in need of a Saviour, repenting of my sins, and welcoming Jesus into my life as Lord and Saviour. Will you make that decision to participate in God's plan for your life today?

If you have never given your life to Jesus or accepted Him as your Lord and Saviour, today is your day.

I invite you to say the following prayer:

> *Dear Lord Jesus,*
> *I am a sinner in need of a Saviour. I believe that You are the Son of God and that You came and died for my sins. I repent of all my sins. I believe that You died on the cross, and on the third day, You rose again, and You ascended, and now You are sitting at the right hand of God, the Father. I accept You as my Lord and Saviour. Wash me in Your blood, forgive me of all my sins. Today, write my name down in the lamb's book of life. Amen.*

If you said this prayer, welcome to the Kingdom of God. Please follow up with water baptism and get plugged into a Bible-believing church that teaches the gospel of Jesus Christ.

Love
Sue-Ann Montaque

About the Author

Sue-Ann Montaque is mother to a teenage son and a proud
Jamaican. In giving her life to Christ, she continues to
serve in her local assembly. She is a speaker, author,
kingdom apparel designer, and minister of the gospel. She
is also the founder of the movement *Jesus Girl Movement
International Limited,* where "It's more than a brand, it's
a movement": a ministry committed to raising up Jesus
Girls of all nations who are passionately uncompromising
in their pursuit of Jesus. With the foundation of building

a network of fellowship and sisterhood, this ministry aims to develop Jesus Girls who will transform the world and those around them through the unearthing and development of their gifts and talents according to Ephesians 4:11-12.

When at home, you can find Sue-Ann spending time with her son and mom, baking and lounging on the beach.

Connect with Sue-Ann Montaque on: